GHOSTS OF THE CALIFORNIA MISSIONS

AND EL CAMINO REAL

RICHARD SENATE

SHORELINE PRESS

Santa Barbara, California

Dedicated to
Brother Tim, OFM
Who told many a ghostly tale
and offered a kind word
when it was most needed.

I would like to thank the following people
for their help with this book.
Monsignor Francis Weber
Rob and Anne Wlodarski
Tom and Julie Watkins
John Anthony Miller
Elizabeth C. Garcia
Ranger Steve Jones
Gloria Truckmann
Joyce Davantzis
Christine Blake
Christy Brown
Jane Gilbert
John Lamb

ISBN: 978-1-885375-23-0

SHORELINE PRESS
P.O. Box 3562
Santa Barbara, CA 93130

Website: ghost-stalker.com. Illustrations are adapted from The Century
Illustrated Monthly Magazine 1889 and 1896 and historical or staff photos.

Table of Contents

Introduction 1
The Phantom Mass 3
My First Ghost 7
Mission San Diego de Alcala 9
The Estudillo Adobe 11
El Campo Santo 13
San Antonia de Pala 15
Mission San Luis Rey de Francia............................ 17
Las Flores Adobe 19
Mission San Juan Capistrano................................. 21
El Adobe de Capistrano 23
Mission San Gabriel Arcángel............................... 25
Avila Adobe, Olvera Street 27
Mission San Fernando Rey de Espana 29
San Fernando's Lost Mine 33
Mission San Buenaventura 35
Ortega Adobe 37
The Haunted Jail 38
Olivas Adobe 39
The Curse of Los Padres Mine 43
Mission Santa Barbara 45
The Old Stone Building 48
De La Guerra Adobe 49
Ghosts of the Painted Cave 51
Haunted Gaviota Pass 53
Mission Santa Inés 55
La Purisima Concepcion 57
Mission San Luis Obispo de Tolosa 61
Mission San Miguel Arcángel 63
Rios-Caledonia Adobe 64
Mission San Antonio de Padua 65
Mission Nuestra Senora de Soledad 67
The Ghosts of Old Monterey 69
Mission San Carlos de Borromeo del Rio Carmelo 71
Mission Santa Cruz 73
Mission Santa Clara de Asis 75
Mission San Jose 77
Mission San Francisco de Asis 79
The Ghosts of Sanchez Adobe 81
Mission San Juan Bautista 82
Mission San Rafael Arcangel 85
Mission Sonoma 86
Father Serra's Lost Mission 87
The Ghosts of the Lost Missions of California 91
Hunting Mission Ghosts 94

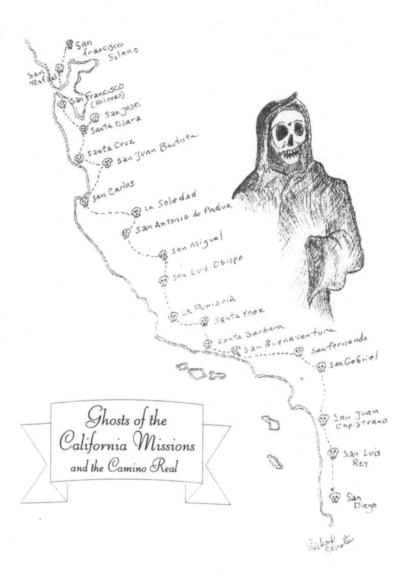

San Francisco Solano
San Rafael
San Francisco (Dolores)
San Jose
Santa Clara
Santa Cruz
San Juan Bautista
San Carlos
La Soledad
San Antonio de Padua
San Miguel
San Luis Obispo
La Purisima
Santa Ynez
Santa Barbara
San Buenaventura
San Fernando
San Gabriel
San Juan Capistrano
San Luis Rey
San Diego

Ghosts of the
California Missions
and the Camino Real

Ghosts of the California Missions and the Camino Real

El Camino Real, the King's Highway, links the twenty-one missions of California. This fabled roadway holds many tales of mystery and wonder. Some of the old missions and adobes are rumored to be haunted; some are believed to hold hidden treasures. Many of the missions harbor mysteries still unsolved. Some of these tales may well be the products of the storyteller's art such as the yarn of the toe sucking vampire of Mission Santa Inez or the ghostly lady in black at the Olivas Adobe. Some accounts may have their roots in fact -- not fantasy. Here are but a few tales of the sometimes mysterious California Missions and the Camino Real.

When the Spanish missionaries came to California in 1769 they came to instill the Christian faith in the natives of this new land. By 1823, the padres had completed twenty-one missions that stretched in a chain from San Diego to Sonoma , some 650 miles! With the decline of the missions in the 1830s and 1840s the padres left and the lands were sold. Slowly the magnificent structures began to deteriorate.

The crumbling ruins along El Camino Real sparked the imagination of the new settlers who arrived after the discovery of gold in 1849. Legends were told around campfires of Spanish gold and phantom monks. So were born the legends and lore of the Kings Highway. The missions and many of the old adobe haciendas have their own unique folklore and tales. Though many of these legends originate years ago, people to this day have their own new experiences adding to these legends. The missions of California are unique place to visit. For thousands of visitors, the missions can be a fascinating place to learn about California's history. For some who follow the King's Highway, their journey will be more of an encounter with history.

The Phantom Mass

Many of the missions have tales of ghostly services held one night each year. The best description of such an encounter is found within Richard Edward White's poem.

...But each year the Padre rises
From his grave the Mass to say,
In the midnight, mid the ruins,
On the eve of San Carlo's day

Then the sad souls, long years buried,
From their lowly graves arise,
And, as if doom's trump had sounded,
Each assumes his mortal guise;

And they come from San Juan's Mission,
From St. Francis by the bay,
From the Mission San Diego,
And the Mission San Jose.

With their gaudy painted banners,
And their flambeaux burning bright,
In a long procession come they
Through the darkness and the night;

Singing hymns and swinging censers,
Dead folks' ghosts they onward pass
To the ivy-covered ruins,
To be present at the Mass.

And the grandsire, and the grand dame,
And their children march along,
And they know not one another
In that weird, unearthly throng.

And the youth and gentle maiden,
They who loved in days of yore,
Walk together now as strangers,
For the dead love nevermore.

In the church now all are gathered,
And not long have they to wait;
From his grave the Padre rises,
Midnight Mass to celebrate.

First he blesses all assembled,
Soldiers, Indians, acolytes;
Then he bows before the altar,
And begins the mystic rites.

When the Padre sings the sanctus,
And the Host is raised on high,
Then the bells up in the belfry,
Swung by spirits, make reply;

And the drums roll, and the soldiers
In the air a volley fire,
While the salutaris rises
Grandly from the phantom choir

"Ite Misa est," is spoken
At the dawning of the day,
And the pageant strangely passes
From the ruins sere and gray;

And Junipero the Padre
Lying down, resumes his sleep,
And the tar-weeds, rank and noisome,
Offer his grave luxuriant creep.

And the lights upon the altar
And the torches cease to burn,
And the vestments and the banners
Into dust and ashes turn;

And the ghostly congregation
Cross themselves, and, one by one,
Into thin air swiftly vanish,
And the midnight Mass is done.

San Carlos de Borromeo, Santa Barbara and San Buenaventura have tales of such ghostly services.

Father Junipero Serra

My First Ghost

During the Summer of 1978 I was taking part in an archaeological field school at Mission San Antonio De Padua in Jolon, California. It is the third mission founded by Father Junipero Serra, dedicated in 1771. Because the mission is so isolated, the nearest town is little more than a tiny hamlet, we students lived amongst the Franciscan monks in the old adobe buildings.

We had been told that the mission was haunted. During the first few weeks of our excavations, I experienced nothing that would indicate this. We were excavating in 105 degree weather under a scorching sun. There was much to do related to the "dig" and lectures filled our evenings.

Several weeks into the process, I had taken on a special project and found myself working late into the night in the small museum. I had lost track of the time. I checked my watch and realized it was time for bed. I closed up the building and walked out into the beautiful courtyard of the mission. I was in the rose garden where an ornate fountain bubbled in the dim light of a waning moon. I walked along the garden path. A strange glow caught my eye. Someone was walking and carrying a flickering candle. The figure moved slowly down the courtyard by the archways. The night was dark and I could clearly see the candlelight illuminating the large dark hallway. I walked on a parallel path in the garden. I wasn't concerned because I believed this to be one of the resident monks or a fellow student carrying the candle. Curious to find out who else was up so late, I changed direction. I drew near and saw it was the figure of a monk with a robe and cowl. I began to move closer but he vanished into thin air! There was no place any living person could have hidden so suddenly. I was completely alone in the dim courtyard. I was confused by what had just happened. Could the image have been my imagination? No, I had watched the light for too long. I could come up with no other explanation. I had encountered my first ghost.

I just could not sleep that night. I left the light on all night. The next day I spoke with a monk at the mission. Brother Tim told me that several other specters had been seen over the years. They include a headless woman who rides a white horse on moonlit nights and vanishes before she reaches the church. There is also a ball of light near a grave in the courtyard where many strange events had taken place.

Troy, a fellow archaeological student, reported seeing a strange light. It came into his room (next to mine) and it pinned him to his bed for a few moments. He was very frightened, but insisted it was only a pinched nerve. After he left, I remember hearing creaks and groans from his empty room.

Brother Tim told us all many the ghost stories about the old mission, but I felt at ease there. I never felt "spooked." Since our experiences there, many others have come forward with stories about the Mission San Antonio. There is a doorway next to the church where only a shadow seems to stand from time to time and a certain area in the mission cemetery that is always much colder than the rest of the cemetery. The place is haunted.

My unexpected encounter was the beginning of my quest to discover the nature of ghosts and the psychic world and I began my search on El Camino Real.

Mission San Diego

This is the first mission established in California. lt was founded by Fray Junipero Serra on July 16, 1769. It was the start of the 21 missions that would be built in the Golden State. It was a mission that almost failed from the start. The founders believed it was an act of God that saved the whole enterprise.

When the expedition of Don Gaspar de Portola and Fray Junipero Serra reached San Diego Bay they were met by two supply ships, the *San Carlos* and the *San Antonio* that had sailed directly from Mexico. Scurvy had taken 60 of the 90 crewmen. One ship was returned for more supplies as the colony suffered from near starvation. In desperation, Portola planned to abandon the expedition and return to Mexico. Fray Junipero convinced him to hold on until the feast of St. Joseph (March 19), the patron saint of the expedition. Portola reluctantly agreed and Serra prayed for the return of the supply ship. On the evening of St. Joseph's Day, the sails of the relief ship were sighted and the project saved. This was seen by the Spanish as a sign from God. They must continue on with the conquest of California.

The story of the mission San Diego would go on to be a sad one. On the night of November 4, 1776 a war party of 800 natives attacked the mission. Fray Luis Jayme courageously marched out to meet the warriors in an attempt to calm the natives. He approached them with his hands empty in a gesture of peace, saying "Love God, my children!" The next day his bloody body was discovered pierced by many arrows. He became California's first martyr. He is buried in the church. It is believed that it is his saintly spirit that wanders the Mission of San Diego to this day. A woman visiting the mission saw a grey-robed form standing near the altar rail inside the church. He smiled at her. She was horrified to see red blotches appearing on his robe as he slowly faded away.

Another witness saw the gray shadow move slowly in the garden area in the late afternoon. She said that the image looked like a man-shaped cloud.

The most persistent of San Diego Mission's ghost tales are of ghostly voices heard in the museum. A woman heard a low mumble, she believed was Spanish, right behind her ear. She doesn't speak Spanish but she distinctly heard the words "Jesus Cristo" and the word "luz" (light). It was a man's voice that spoke softly and slowly in an almost musical tone. Another visitor heard a voice as she was looking into a display depicting a padre's sleeping quarters. The voice said only "familia?" It was almost like a question.

Cold spots and chills have frequently been reported near the entrance of the church. Perhaps it is the ghost of Fray Luis Jayme, the padre who gave his life for this church that watches over the Mission San Diego even still.

He, who loves not the voices of the past, should not find entrance here;

It serves him best who seeks alone to walk and meditate.

His past-evoking musings unconfessed.

"Mission San Diego"
Minnie M. Tingle

Mission San Diego
10818 San Diego Mission Road. Open daily from 9 to 5.

The Estudillo Adobe

This Adobe is restored now as a museum. It stands in quiet dignity in San Diego's Old Town Historic Park. If the stories of visitors and staff are correct, this 1829 adobe is not at peace. It is one of the more haunted sites on the Camino Real.

Visitors tell of misty figures in the chapel room, figures that have the shape of a Spanish padre with robe and cowl. Still other accounts tell of ghostly faces appearing in the mirrors, strange music wafting through and cold chambers, even on warm days!

The ghosts seem to be offended by photographers. Several cameras have been affected over the last three decades. Visitors find odd things like orbs of light in the pictures after they are developed. A group of investigators were "forced-out" of the mission when they attempted to do their research and photography a few years ago. Where the past and present meet, anything can happen.

While visiting Old Town be sure to stop in at the old Whaley House just two blocks away. It is said to be the most haunted house in California. Built in 1857, this two-story structure has served as a residence, courthouse and theater. The house lives up to its haunted reputation with icy cold spots, phantom cigar smells and rocking chairs that rock themselves! The ghosts are believed to be Thomas Whaley, his long-suffering wife Anna, their two children, the sad ghost of Annabelle Washburn (a neighbor child who died in a tragic accident) and last, but not least, the small dark dog owned by the Whaley Family. These ghosts are said to make themselves known in the house or on the grounds with alarming regularity.

Both sites are "must-see" and fall seems to be the best time for ghost hunting!

Estudillo Adobe is located at 4002 Wallace Avenue just off the Old Town Plaza. Whaley House stands on the corner of Harney and San Diego Avenue. 2482 San Diego Avenue, Old Town.

" Gentlemen,
I ask your pardon for all my offenses
and give you mine in return."

Quote by Antonio Garra
Native American leader of the bloody uprising of
1852 before his execution at the Campo Santo.

El Campo Santo

This adobe walled burial place was established in 1849 and is where many of the leading citizens of San Diego lie buried, including the mischievous Yankee Jim Robinson (who is also rumored to haunt the nearby Whaley House). It's a gloomy place even on the warmest days, and it takes on a spooky atmosphere at night. Tales of ghosts at El Campo Santo have been circulating for a century. Several icy cold spots and drifting apparitions have been encountered here.

Stories tell of a phantom gunfighter in the small cemetery late at night. Legend identifies the ghost as Antonio Garra, a Native American chief who was shot by firing squad and buried at the site in 1852. There is also an apparition of a woman in a low-cut dress and long skirt with a bandanna on her head. Her translucent image stands outside the gate. A psychic believed she was the ghost of a lady of the night who was forbidden burial with the decent folks and given a simple grave outside the sacred grounds. Now her unhappy spirit longs to be buried with the others.

"In 2001 my girlfriend and I were walking by the Old Cemetery at Old Town talking about the ghosts when we saw this thing drift from the back of the Cemetery. It was all white and like a… sort of cloud. It moved at the speed of a fast walk. I believe it was a woman, don't ask how I know, I just got that impression. It was the creepiest thing I have ever seen. … It was about the size of a small woman. No, we were not drinking…"

Name withheld by request

El Campo Santo
2400 block of San Diego Avenue, Old Town San Diego.

*"It was hot that day, I remember that much... It was
in the late afternoon. We had just walked into the
courtyard of the Mission (San Antonio) when we saw
a patch of mist in the shade of the archway. It had
the shape of a man but it looked like steam. It was
whitish gray and it started to move out towards the
fountain and then it was just gone. I had the distinct
impression it was the spirit of a padre...I never
believed in ghosts until I saw that..."*
Name with held at request of witness

San Antonio de Pala - The Last True Mission

Most people think of the California Missions as Twenty-One stations along the coast. there were two on the Colorado River as well. The truth is that there was also a chain of smaller branch missions spaced between the main mission outposts. These asistencias served the spiritual needs of Native People too far from the missions to receive daily instruction otherwise. Most of these smaller establishments are long gone or exist only as place names such as Santa Paula, San Marcos and Santa Clarita.

Two of the asistencia survive today. One San Bernardino is now a museum in the California city of the same name. The other is the only mission that still fulfills its designated purpose by serving as a Native American Church for the Community at the Pala Indian Reservation north of San Diego. The Church was built in 1816 and is best known for its attractive Bell Wall. Several notable people lie buried in the small cemetery of the church.

Visitors tell of a ghostly padre wandering the grounds, still looking after the parish he once served. One fellow came to the branch mission with a tape recorder and spent time in the cemetery and chapel. When he played back the audio tape he heard a soft ghostly voice say " Madre de Dio."

Another near-by branch mission is now gone. The Santa Isabel adobe chapel was built in 1818 and a modern church stands on the site. One of the enduring mysteries of California concerns two bells purchased by the Native Converts of Santa Isabel. They were stolen in the 1920s and remain lost to this day. Legends say that the bells have supernatural qualities. One story has it they were retrieved by the natives themselves and are still hidden in a cave in the nearby mountains.

Mission San Antonio de Pala
Pala Mission Road. Pala, California
(760) 742-1600

15

Still stands the cloistered mystery,
whose wasted walls enfold.
Vast stories of hidden history
unwritten or untold.
"San Luis Rey"
B.C. Corby

Mission San Luis Rey

This impressive mission was founded by Fray Fermin Lasuen on June 13, 1798 as the 18th mission in California. This mission became one of the most prosperous. If there is a ghost padre at this mission, it might well be the venerable Antonio Peyri. For 34 years Peyri labored to build San Luis Rey into a success. When he was called to Spain in 1832, the Native American converts followed him to the ship in San Diego trying to convince him to stay. For years they placed flowers and candles before a picture of Peyri preferring to pray to a Saint they knew rather than ones they had been told about. He died in Spain. Perhaps he visits the mission where he labored so long and visits with the spirits of the people he came to love as his own family.

Many ghostly stories are about hearing moaning and seeing a faceless monk who wanders the grounds around midnight. It is said that the bells in the tower ring 13 times when he appears. Those unlucky enough to encounter this figure and look into his empty hood are driven insane! Legend says he was murdered by unfriendly tribesmen long ago and now haunts the mission grounds. The basis for the tale isn't found in the ancient records of the church and there isn't a single reference to any padres at this mission falling victim to Native American wrath. The root of this tale is found in Walt Disney's TV show, Zorro! In one of the half-hour programs the masked hero, Zorro, saved a man hiding in the church by pretending to be a ghost! He told the superstitious Spanish soldiers the yarn of the murdered priest to frighten them so he could save the person in the church. That episode of the popular series was filmed at Mission San Luis Rey and could be the source of the ghostly tale today. Still several people swear they have seen the apparition near the cemetery and walking in front of the church! They never see his face (which may be a good thing, if the story has any truth at all.) Many have heard moaning in the old sunken garden where legend says the padre met his grim end.

17

Could these accounts be just fabrications of minds influenced by Hollywood or could it be that the TV story was based on a legend of forgotten historical events? Perhaps the images of the forgotten murdered monk are awful memories trapped in time and space to play over and over like an endless loop of a television rerun.

Perhaps the sightings of the padre are real, faint images from the past of such an influential man as Fray Antonio Peyri. We say in Spanish "Quien sabe?" (Who knows?)

The mission is well worth a visit because of its many rare artifacts and its high dome over the altar. I visited the place on a cold wet afternoon, and the atmosphere of the place seemed to reek of the past. If you can, visit the place on a cool winter's day, and tour the old sunken gardens as well. Who knows? Maybe you will chance upon the dark-robed monk. If you do, be sure to avert your eyes from his face, and do ask his name: Como se llama? Mission San Luis Rey is located at 4050 Mission Avenue, Oceanside.

Las Flores Adobe

In 1865, early California pioneer Marco Forster built the Las Flores adobe on Rancho Santa Margarita, near the San Pedro Estancia. It was once part of Camp Pendleton in Oceanside but it is now owned by the Boy Scouts of America. It also has a long reputation of being haunted.

A young man heard the distinct sounds of a horse neighing late at night. There were no horses in the area. Another account tells of two women living in the adobe who saw a pair of robed padres right in their bedroom! The women were frightened speechless by the ghosts. The disembodied Franciscans sensed their distress and said "Be calm, my children." and then seemed to "float"away. Adobe legend explains the ghostly monks as the restless spirits of two padres who were captured and tortured to death by enraged natives.

Years ago a Marine corporal saw a man walking the site in a brown robe and speaking in a language other than English. As the soldier watched, the robed stranger then vanished into thin air. There are accounts of a ghost woman who wanders the upper rooms of the house; it is said that a woman died of a long illness in the house long ago. The ranch now serves as a Boy Scout camp. As more and more visitors come, the stories of the ghosts of Las Flores might well increase.

A registered historic landmark, the Boy Scouts of America developed a Scout camp on the property in 1974. Today, Rancho Las Flores is used by thousands of Scouts and other youth groups.

19

Fell the bells with crashing tower.
When the Temblor shook the earth;
Then the men in startled terror,
Fled the church and comrades dearth.

"Bells of Capistrano"
Clarice Garland

Mission San Juan Capistrano

Founded by Fray Junipero Serra November 1, 1776, this mission prospered in the early years (between 1797 and 1806) so well that an ambitious cruciform stone church was built. On the night of December 8, 1812, a terrible earthquake destroyed the stone church, taking the lives of forty worshipers. This massive ruin is all that remains of the Padres' dream. The tragedy has forever scarred the site and the ghostly happenings are directly linked to the disaster.

The best known phantom is a lady in a long white dress. She carries a candle through the ruins of the stone church. The legend says she was one of the many victims of the terrible earthquake. She was killed before she could confess her sins and now wanders, doomed, until she can at long last seek confession. But this sad specter isn't alone. Some witnesses have reported encountering a black-shrouded woman, dressed in the style of Spanish Californian, standing under the last archway of the northern corner of the mission complex. One tale tells of haunted bells that toll by themselves whenever a good person dies.

The most enduring legend of San Juan Capistrano is that of the return of the swallows. They are held to return on St. Joseph's Day each year to rebuild their nests among the adobe ruins. Many of the birds arrive days before the appointed time and others come later, and all are greeted by camera-bearing tourists. The romantic story of the swallows has become a sort of cottage industry for the mission community with news crews and reporters flocking to the hamlet on the prescribed day. It is believed that fewer of the birds show up than in mission day because the land around the mission that once supplied the birds with food in the form of insects has been subdivided and developed. But the birds always return to San Juan Capistrano and so do many visitors. It is a very beautiful mission and a truly lovely community to visit and viewing the swallows is still a real joy.

Several years ago a team of psychic investigators went over the mission seeking evidence that the old place was haunted. In one experiment they placed a tape recorder in the graveyard and let it run. There was no one present but, upon re-winding the tape they discovered a faint voice saying "I'm so cold." and "Help me!" An interesting feature was that the voice was in English rather than Spanish or a Native American language. Could the spirit be from the 20th Century, and not the distant past? Walk the grounds of the cemetery silently, respectfully, ever mindful of a whispered sound.

The most haunting story I have ever heard regarding San Juan Capistrano was told to me by a former employee of the mission gift shop. One rainy day, when the place was nearly deserted, a woman in a white dress came walking silently into the shop. The shop is located in what was once the original padres quarters of the mission. The woman, who looked Latina, had long jet-black hair. The witness said she looked confused and perhaps ill. Her skin was deathly pale. The clerk approached the woman and asked if she needed help. The strange woman didn't speak. She looked around then silently walked right directly through a thick adobe wall! It had been raining and the woman appeared wet but there were no footprints upon the floor. Who was she? Why was she present? Perhaps she was seeking one of the padres. Maybe the apparition was the famed woman in white still seeking a Father for confession? The gift shop is a must see for anyone seeking the ghosts of San Juan Capistrano.

Mission San Juan Capistrano is located at
the corner of Camino Capistrano and
Ortega Highway and worth seeing!
Open daily from 8:30 to 5. Fee to enter.

El Adobe de Capistrano

Built in 1830 as a courthouse, this adobe is now a famed restaurant featuring mariachi music, margaritas and enchiladas that President Nixon loved. The old place is also haunted.

Below the rooms that once served as a courtroom, is the dark and grim jail where malefactors were held. This cell has been converted into the wine cellar and it is a fitting place to keep wines because it is always cold down there. Long ago, a waiter went into the wine cellar and saw a hand print appear on a dusty bottle of vino as if an invisible hand had placed its palm and fingers on the dark bottle. A psychic visited the room and saw the apparition of a man with matted hair and a bloody face appear in the dim room. Indeed a cold and foreboding atmosphere clings under the building.

It is well worth a visit and the food is surprisingly good. Mr. Nixon did know good Mexican food.

El Adobe de Capistrano is located at 31891 Camino Capistrano.

Still seems to brood above that structure olden,
The spirit of a past long laid in dust;--
low winds of balm, shine sun rays warm and golden
Keep these quaint walls in trust!

"Mission San Gabriel"
Sylvia Lawson Corey

Mission San Gabriel

Founded September 8, 1771, San Gabriel is the fourth Mission. The church is built of stone and is said to be a loving but crude copy of a Moorish style cathedral in Cordova, Spain. The supernatural played a role in the founding of the place. One legend claims that a group of natives yelling and making war-like gestures approached the founding party. One of the friars unrolled a large painting of the virgin. At the sight of the painting the natives tossed down their weapons and placed their necklaces before the image. The painting estimated at over 300 years old still hangs in the church.

This mission one is also rumored to be haunted. A ghostly Native American, all dressed in white with a blanket and long hair, drifts along the wall of the church. He is searching for his lost love, who died just days before they were to be wed. The ghost is seen when the old bells ring. The large Angelus Bell that hangs in the bell wall, or Campanario, is dated 1830, and weighs over a ton. It is said that on a clear day its tone can be heard in Los Angeles, eight miles away. Perhaps the ghostly convert was a bell ringer long ago and misses the music of the bells.

When you visit this mission, be sure to see a unique set of the stations of the cross painted by an unknown Indian artist. The artist may have placed a political message in his 14 works. He depicted Christ as an Indian and the Roman soldiers persecuting him are dressed as Spanish Lancers. These works originally hung in San Fernando Mission and were painted on sailcloth purchased from trade ships.

Mission San Gabriel , 428 South Mission Drive San Gabriel.
Open daily from 9 to 4.

Avila Adobe, Downtown Los Angeles

The Sepulveda House, Downtown Los Angeles

The Avila Adobe, Olvera Street

The city of Los Angeles began here in 1781 It is now a cultural center and tourist stop with many shops and attractions. It perhaps has some of the best Mexican restaurants in the area and is known for its many celebrations, from the Blessing of the Animals to the Day of the Dead. Many stories of ghosts seemed to be linked to the 1818 Avila Adobe, where John C. Fremont made his headquarters after taking Los Angeles in the Mexican-American War. A dark form is said to hover in the yard of the building and footsteps are heard in the restored rooms. One psychic told me that she was propelled out of the house by invisible hands while touring the place. If there is a ghost, it might be that of the builder owner of the place, Don Francisco Avila. There are many reasons why the modest adobe would be haunted. In the days of Spanish and Mexican rule it was the site for many hot meetings . It is said that Jose Maria Avila was the ringleader for many plots to overthrow the government. In time the house was given the unique nickname: "*La Casa Revolucionaria*".

Others ghosts and supernatural events are reported in the old Sepulveda House (built in 1887.) There the spirit of an elderly lady, all dressed in black and holding a jet black set of rosary beads, is said to walk. The 1884 fire station, just off Olvera Street on Sanchez, is haunted by a fireman who is rumored to have lost his life fighting an early fire. Sometimes they smell the smoke from his pipe as he waits for the final bell that will send his weary soul to the great firehouse in the sky.

Avila Adobe and the Casa Sepulveda are located
near a mexican marketplace with shops and restaurants
in a very historic part of Los Angeles, a real must see!
Avila Adobe, 10 Olvera Street, Downtown Los Angeles.
The Sepuveda House, 622 North Main, Downtown Los Angeles.

Misión San Fernando Rey de España

Mission San Fernando

Founded September 8, 1797, by Fray Fermin Lasuen as California's seventeenth mission. One of the major activities of San Fernando was ranching. In its prime, this mission owned over 12,800 head of cattle. It became known for the intricate leather work done there. A case could be made that this mission is perhaps one of the most haunted in Southern California.

The best known story at this site is one that finds its roots in the modern age. The phantom is that of an elderly woman but, unlike many ghosts, this figure is surrounded by her spectral pet cats. That's why she is known as "cat woman." The story holds that she liked to feed the many stray cats that found a home at the mission. Even in historic times, cats were an important part of the mission life, because they kept down the population of mice and rats. She would clean the long archway of the convento building and there leave food for the many felines she loved. They say she would talk to them and comfort the animals. Many saw her as a harmless eccentric. The mission fathers tolerated her because she kept the place clean. In time, like all before her, she went to her reward. But from that day on, people swear they have seen her apparition walking the archway and park surrounded by troops of phantom cats. These supernatural creatures are loyal even beyond death and have frightened away dogs. Even large police dogs are said to whimper and flee with their tails between their legs when they encounter the woman and her cats. But if "cat woman" wanders, she is likely joined by many others.

Even the massive ornate fountain at this mission is believed to be haunted. It is shaped like a Moorish star, and is a copy of one in Cordova, Spain. The water is said to turn to blood before an assassination of a national leader or great disaster. It is said to have turned red when John F. Kennedy was shot in Dallas, Texas.

Many have felt the presence of a padre in the old library, and heard (and smelled) things in the wine cellar.

One legend states that a tunnel linked the Mission to the Andre Pico Adobe located almost a mile away. That two-storied adobe home is rumored to be haunted by the ghost of Catarina Pico. A photograph of a person with a dark shadow is displayed in the library. Could this be the ghost? This fine adobe was badly damaged in the earthquake of January, 1994.

A letter from visitors to the mission who had experiences at the Mission San Fernando:

Well, we were nearly the only ones at the Mission. In the convento, there were sounds of gates opening and closing. Even sometimes a gate we had closed and was right behind us. We'd run to investigate, and there would be no sign of anyone or any gate in the convento. On the stairs in the convento that lead to an upstairs room, there were visible to the naked eye, orange orbs. When I climbed the stairs to get a feel, it seemed like heat was radiating off the wall. I had my friend feel over the wall and he felt it too. But the wall itself was cold. Then from inside the room, which was locked, came loud banging sounds. Sometimes when walking through rooms I smelled burning wood, freshly chopped wood, and/ or some kind of incense. In the room with the flat topped canopy, my friend saw a cloaked figure shadow, creep by. We then heard music, and followed it. It was playing in the Madonna room. There is a motion sensor that plays the music. But, at the time, no one was in the convento but us. And we didn't walk in the room. By the library outside of it... we both sensed something cold in the corner. Then, were the wine cellar is, we saw white haziness by the door. It was weird cause we went to the rectory and met a lady that worked there that confirmed a ghost hunters club had come out and said there were 3 ghosts by the upstairs thing, 1 ghost that hung out in that corner, and some on the stairs in the wine cellar. She confirmed our paranoia. Her name was

Loretta, I believe. She, too, spoke of places she didn't like going in the mission. But I really, really was curious about a female ghost, that I think I had come into contact with. Which is why I asked about the Ranch. Me and my friend both heard her whispers. The whole experience is odd. I went there, because my house is haunted. And, I figured, since I am in walking distance to the mission, that the mission has something to do with it. So if I can figure out its secrets, then I can figure out the secrets of my own property, and know how to deal/understand it all. Thank you for your help.

Mission San Fernando is located at 15151 San Fernando Mission Blvd., San Fernando.

31

Reyes Adobe Ghost

Built by Jose Jacinto Reyes in 1850 this landmark adobe stands today in the city of Agoura Hills, restored and open as a museum of the Rancho Era in California History. It was used as a horse ranch for many years but remained vacant for decades while it was restored. It opened to the public in 2002. Stories of ghosts at the old house remained constant.

One story tells of the day a brazen bandit broke into the house in day light. The men were away at the time, as was frequently the case on a working cattle ranch. The bandit seized Mrs. Reyes. In the struggle, she somehow drew his own pistol and shot him. It is said that after the body was taken out of the kitchen by the other women at the house, she continued her job of cooking, as if nothing had happened! They buried the man somewhere on the grounds, (possibly in the manure pit) not speaking of the event, fearing the dead man's outlaw friends might seek revenge for his death. Perhaps it is the bandit who still haunts the house. This is a story they do not tell to the school children who visit the adobe on field trips, but one that underlines the truth that the 19th Century was a time more lawless than our own! People with a psychic gift say they feel the ghosts want to tell their story and welcome all who visit them in the spirit of hospitality.

> *" (I have) been there about seven times... (I) got two women (and) a strong male ... Main house and barn are loaded (with) orbs and dark shadows in main house... Sunset is great (there) ... saw a blue orb float between the barn and house.... amazing.. (and I) saw what looked like a candle move in the house... (the) women are both short.. one may be a cook for the family... (the) man is strong.. like an 'El Jefe' (The Chief or Boss)...."*

Rob Wlodarski Author
psychic investigator

Reyes Adobe Historical Site
5464 Reyes Adobe Road, Agoura Hills, CA 91303
(818) 597-7361

San Fernando Mission's Lost Mine

Mission convert Rojerio Rocha was the silversmith at the mission San Fernando in the last days of the Mission era. Not only was he well known for his skills in working precious metals but he also played the violin at the Mass. He knew where the Spanish Padre's worked a mine up Pacoima Creek.

American bandits came to where he lived one day and he was badly beaten and his wife was killed. He vowed that the mission treasure would never go to the "Godless Ones." Near his death in 1904 his greedy son talked him into making a map to mark the way to the lost mine. The son had a sheep skin brought to his death bed and with a hot poker he drew the map including many Native American and Catholic mission symbols. He did this so only a Native would be able to follow the arrows to the buried mine. He had his son vow to never show the map to the Yankees and then the old man died. Soon after his burial the son went to a local saloon and sold the map to Americans. They followed the directions as close as they could up the canyon and to a large tree. They dig down for twenty feet but found nothing.

Many believe that Native American Symbols still at the mission must be consulted to crack the code and find the lost mine. Some say the treasure is cursed and guarded by the unhappy spirit of Rocha who will strike out at any Yankee who seeks the lost mine. Most agree that the silver mine is there with a bounty of silver waiting for a worthy prospector.

*Mission San Buenaventura,
211 East Main St., Ventura
The mission is located near
an art and history museum
and interesting shops and
restaurants, and all steps from
the Pacific Ocean. A California
experience, a real must!*

Mission San Buenaventura

Founded March 31, 1782, by Fray Junipero Serra as the ninth and last mission he would establish. The present church was completed in 1809, and reconstructed after the destructive earthquake of 1812. One unique feature is the three bells made of wood that once hung in the bell tower. Two remain and are the only examples of wooden bells in the Americas. The exact purpose for their carving remains a mystery. Two exact replicas were carved several years ago and will be displayed.

Rumors from the 1880s tell the story of a phantom monk, all in gray, who wanders the grounds of the mission. There are many stories and encounters told of this persistent padre. One story tells that a woman with a problem paying her rent spent time at the church, even giving up her last dollars to the poor box. When she left the church, she saw a monk who walked toward her with a smile. As she watched the figure vanished away. When she returned home, there was a check in her mailbox from a man who had borrowed money from her a decade before. It was enough to pay her rent with extra for food. Another account tells of a woman who was praying that her husband would return to the church after many years. He was suffering from cancer and she believed a renewal of faith might help him in this battle for his life. As she prayed she saw a monk standing behind her. She got up to speak with him, but he walked out the door. When she got to the courtyard there was no one there. She walked to the rectory and asked the priest where was the visiting monk. He informed her there wasn't any. He asked her to describe the figure. When she told him of the gray robes the priest laughed. "You have seen our ghost!" he said. The story goes that when she returned home, her husband informed her that he had changed his mind, and would go to Mass the next Sunday. The woman believed that the phantom monk somehow, supernaturally, caused her husband to change his mind.

One woman touring the mission with her family saw the ghost monk standing under a tree in the courtyard. She walked up and started to tell him that, even though she wasn't a Roman Catholic, she found the mission church charming. She asked if he would give them a tour of the place. She saw her family coming out the side door and motioned for them to join her. When she looked back toward the monk, he had vanished away. Her family walked up and asked why she had been talking to herself. From this we can deduce that the phantom monk doesn't do tours. The ghost monk is thought to be one of the three early padres who established the mission and now lay buried beside the altar. Some whisper that the figure is an "unknown saint" sent by the grace of God to watch over the parish and help those in need.

Confessional and pulpit inside
Mission San Buenaventura.

Ortega Adobe

This middle class adobe home in one of the last 19th Century houses of its type still standing in California. Built in 1857 by local rancher Emedigio Ortega he raised nine of his children in the small three room house. It was here in 1897 that one of his sons began the Ortega Chili Company that exists today. The building was used as a Mexican restaurant, a Chinese laundry, a pottery shop, an employment agency, a VFW hall, a speakeasy, the Ventura police station, and lastly, a boys and girl's club. In the 1960s it was opened as a historic museum. The tiles on the roof were purchased from the Old Mission San Buenaventura after the earthquake of 1857.

Supernatural events are part of job for the crew of the adobe museum. Staff have caught a glimpse of a man with a derby hat standing on the porch. A visitor who believes she has a psychic gift saw a ghostly little girl in the house standing in the doorway. She had a dark shawl over her head. The house also has a real cold spot in the largest room where some have heard voices! The stories of soft music emanating from a phantom guitar remind us of the history and many different lives that have passed through this house and of some spirits that may have stayed!

Ortega Adobe Historic Residence
214 West Main Street, Ventura, California
Open daily, Free of Charge

The Haunted Jail

One half block west of the Mission San Buenaventura, on Valdez Alley, stands the vault like brick structure known as "El Caballo." It was a water purification unit built by the Spanish padres in the early years of the 19th Century. It was the terminus for an elaborate aqueduct that spanned seven miles. The water was treated with sand and charcoal before traveling in underground clay pipes to the fountains of the mission, where it provided drinking water to the native converts. After the mission was sold, the aqueduct was damaged, and the water building was abandoned in 1866. When the city of Ventura was incorporated, the little brick building was used as the first city jail. The ghost that hovered in and near the structure dates from this time. In the Spring of 1869, a local man named Lucas Garcia was arrested and accused of murder. The victim's body was found at Garcia's adobe buried in a shallow grave. The dead man's things were found on Garcia's person. The local city lawman left town traveling to Santa Barbara to seek instructions from the county courthouse (Ventura was part of Santa Barbara County at the time). While he was away a mob of local citizens marched up to the little jail, shot off the lock and pulled a screaming Garcia from the building. He was taken to a tall tree on the corner of Main and Ventura Avenue, and there he was lynched. Legends say that screams of "innocent" are said to issue from the old jail building late at night. One man walked up to the bars of the door and cried out, "Garcia, Lucas Garcia, are you there?" and a low moan answered him back. Others say the area around the small building has a persistent cold spot, near the rear window.

Building located on Valdez Alley, near Eastwood Park.

The Olivas Adobe

The 1847 adobe of Don Raymundo Olivas is perhaps one of the most haunted places in all of California. Since it was opened in 1972, the apparition of a woman in a long 19th Century black dress has been encountered by staff and visitors alike. She is seen looking out the windows on the second floor, as well as walking the long balconies at night. She may well be the unhappy ghost of Dona Teodora Olivas, who was the mother of 21 children. It is thought the ghost might be that of one of the daughters who died at the house. This two storied adobe home served as the main house for the vast Rancho San Miguel, and was the social center of the Santa Clara River Valley.

The adobe has a fine collection of artifacts that includes an 1850s era music box (barrel piano) that plays eight songs. Visitors say that the machine sometimes supernaturally plays by itself on cold days. The adobe was once featured on the Fox TV program, "Sightings" in which a team of psychic researchers came away convinced that this house was indeed haunted.

In 2000, a group visiting the adobe at night saw a bright light in the second floor Children's Room. This was the room used by the daughters in the family long ago. As they watched, the light became the apparition of a little girl wearing a white nightgown and cap. The gown was long sleeved with a touch of lace at the collar and she had two long pigtails. She looked at the group, then, the ghost spun around in a pirouette and vanished. There were no projectors or mirrors to account for the strange sightings. The girl has also been seen looking out the window on the second floor as well. It is believed that the ghost might be Maria Olivas, the daughter of Nicholas Olivas, who died as a child at the adobe.

In June of 2006 a group of would be ghost hunters visited the Olivas Adobe and attempted to communicate with the ghostly Lady in Black. They developed a code, using dowsing rods, to answer "Yes" and "No" questions. They conducted this odd séance in the children's room on the second floor. From the answers given by the rods the ghostly woman is Rebecca Olivas De La Riva who grew up in the house and had five of her six children here. Asked if she could show herself to prove her existence a 19th Century nightgown, on one of the beds as a display, jumped off the bed onto the floor!

Dear Sir,

My family and I visited the adobe in Ventura on the afternoon of February 24, 1999. My daughter was studying the history of California at the time, and we thought that it would be a fun place to see on our trip. As we drove up to the place, we observed a woman standing on the balcony of the house dressed in what we thought was a historic costume. She didn't seem to notice us, but her movements and actions seemed to indicate she was upset about something. She was pacing on the balcony. We parked the car and walked toward the building, still watching the woman, when she just vanished. We asked the docent on duty, and we were told that the balcony in the front of the house isn't used these days. It was a mysterious thing.

- Tom and Julie Watkins

To whom it may concern:

"I was locking up, by myself on a rainy Saturday afternoon. It was about four o'clock.

When I got to the chapel (on the second floor) I had the strangest feeling that there was someone else in the room. I sensed he was a young man, maybe 17 or 18 years old. It was so real I turned to look and saw nothing there. I felt like I was intruding on something I shouldn't have. I didn't see anything but the impression was so strong I still get goose bumps thinking of it."

Ms Betsy Havensten

Former Docent

" I was about nine years old and visiting the adobe on an
early Saturday morning. There were only three people there,
including myself. The house was locked up and had not opened
for the day. I was in the courtyard and looked up to the
window on the second floor into the children's room. I saw a
little girl with chestnut brown hair, down to her shoulders, a
white Mop cap, and a white nightgown with a tiny pink bow.
She looked at me and did a sort of double take and when I
blinked, she was gone. When the house was opened there was
no one in the rooms. I wasn't really scared by it, oddly enough.
I had a feeling that she wanted to be a friend."

Megan Shanna.

Olivas Adobe is located at 4200 Olivas Park Drive.
Open Saturday and Sunday 10 am to 4 pm.

The Curse of the Lost Padres Mine

The legends associated with lost gold and silver mines worked by
the Mission Fathers could fill a separate book. Such tales have
their roots in Mexico and may based on mining conducted by the
Jesuit Order in their many missions. Almost every California
Mission has a story or two of lost treasure and a hidden mine.
Perhaps the most intriguing Lost Mine story deals with the one
rumored worked by the padre's of Mission San Buenaventura.
Of all the stories – this one might be true.

The legend starts out with a Mission Native American presenting
the padre with a handful of gold nuggets. The natives lead the
Spanish to a spot where a ledge of gold was exposed in the
headwaters of the Piru Creek. The Padre's then, according to the
tale, had Mission Converts work the mine, tunneling deep within
the mountain. Near the entrance to the mine they built an adobe
chapel so the workers would not need to travel far to attend Mass.
Mule trains carried out the ore where it was held for special ships,
chartered by the Jesuits, to process the gold and send it to Rome.
When the priests were recalled to Europe they closed the mine,
and demolished the chapel. The entrance was hidden and the
Native Chumash workers called together. They were told a
terrible curse was placed upon the mine. This gold was not for
greedy Yankees or selfish Mexican settlers. This gold was only for
his Holiness, the Pope in Rome. Anyone who would come to the
mine to take away some gold for themselves would be struck
down by the awful curse.

Some say that the leaders of the Chumash People today know the
general location of the lost gold mine but warn others away
knowing that to come within five miles of the place will activate
the curse and dire misfortune. One young man, part Native
American, went with his friends up the Piru to pan for gold. Every
year, after big rain storms, an accomplished placer miner can
wash out "color" from the sand. The young man's grandfather

warned him not to go out of fear the curse would lash out at him. He only dismissed the story as a folk tale. Then, one weekend he and his friends moved their camp a mile north, in the move, the young man slipped, fell down a cliff and broke his leg in three places. He had to taken out of the wilderness by a helicopter! While he was recovering at Saint John's Hospital in Oxnard, his grandfather came and told him the "accident" it was a warning-- the next time he went up the Piru Creek he wouldn't come back alive!

He still doesn't believe in the curse, but the young man never returned to the area, just in case.

The lost mine is said to be above
Lake Piru, in the Condor bird sanctuary,
at the beginning of the Piru Creek.
It is rough country and not for beginning hikers.

Mission Santa Barbara

They call this place the Queen of the Missions. When you walk the grounds, one can understand why it has earned this distinction. It is a magnificent building, the only one in the mission chain to have two bell towers. Founded December 4, 1786, by Fray Fermin Lasuen as the 10th mission in California, it is the first mission founded after the death of Fray Junipero Serra. There is a ghostly, haunted side to this Mission as well.

In 1929 one of those twin towers fell down and extensive repairs had to be made. During work a unusual mural was uncovered. Oddly, it was painted in a spot where it would be illuminated by the sun one day out of the year. The mural was made by Indian converts and depicts a cross and two pennants atop a wavy line. It has been interpreted by some to depict the power of the church and state that was built on the back of the Indians. These symbols may have been used to undermine raise support for undermining the padres. In 1824 a bloody revolt swept through three missions.

One contemporary story tells of two visitors to the mission late at night. They report seeing a padre come out of the church, his hands were covered in blood. He went directly to the 1808 fountain and plunged his hands into the water. The entire fountain turned red with gore! The padre suddenly vanished and the fountain returned to normal. Could this padre's spirit symbolically be washing his hands of any guilt in the revolt?

The facade of the mission is unique because it was copied from a book authored by the pagan Roman, Vitruvius. It is based upon a pagan temple to Venus, Goddess of Love. A copy of this book can be seen in the mission library. The three statues that grace the top of the facade are Faith, Hope and Charity. They are believed to be the first statues carved in California, and they were made by the Native converts. The originals are cared for inside in a special room.

A student from Brooks Institute for Photography came to take pictures of the three worn statues. He set up his large-format camera and began to take pictures. The moment he started, he felt an uneasy chill, as if he was being watched. When he looked around there was no one there. He tried to shake off the feeling, but jusr couldn't. When he approached the statues, he felt a distinct push on his shoulders forcing him to kneel before the images! When he looked again, there was nothing there.

A group of psychic investigators toured the Santa Barbara Mission with special cameras and tape recorders. When they entered the church, they were immediatly filled with the feeling that something was there. Here is where many lie buried before the altar. Along side of the altar, in a standing position, are the mortal remains of California's first bishop, Fr. Moreno. A member of the group went to the ornate baptismal font. When he looked into the holy water, he saw a face at the bottom of the basin. At first he thought it was a fancy carving of a cherub until, as he watched amazed, it changed into the face of an old man with a beard. When the image vanished, he dipped his finger into the holy water. He said it felt heavy like lead. Though he isn't a member of the Roman Catholic Church, he felt compelled by something invisible and powerful to make the sign of the cross. He left the church and went out to the cemetery. The Roman arched cemetery doorway is decorated with skulls and crossed bones. Originally the skulls were not carvings but real human bones this was a common decorative device found in churches in Mexico.

In the cemetery the remains of 4000 Indians are buried, and ghosts are seen, felt and heard at this place. Here lie the remains of Juana Maria, known as the lone woman of San Nicholas island. She was left behind when the Indian population was evacuated from the island and she lived alone for 18 years. She lived only a few weeks after being rescued and taken to Santa Barbara. Maybe she is one of the ghosts that are said to wander the old cemetery as the day blends into dusk. A photographer took a picture of a dark shape floating over the tombstone. The form was the shape of an angel, but all in black. Many audio tapes made here have recorded eerie voices, including one in French. When the tape was replayed, a strange voice said simply "Merci." This mission is not only a beautiful and exciting place to visit, some of the spirits are very polite.

I've been meaning to write to you for a year about an interesting paranormal event I had at Santa Barbara Mission. I first became acquainted with your work through your book, "The Haunted Southland," which I have read and re-read. .....On April 10th, 1999, I was driving up to my sister's place in the San Francisco Bay Area, when I decided to stop and visit Santa Barbara Mission. I hadn't been there since a family vacation in 1969. I didn't feel anything until I went into the church itself and knelt in the front pew on the left side. I started getting the feeling that I was in someone's spot, and that "someone" was not pleased that I was there. The antagonistic feeling was so intense that I started to get the urge to just get up and run away. But I suppressed the urge and asked it in Spanish, "excuse me, but who are you?" I then apologized in English for intruding on its space, and told it that sinners had a right to be in church too. I sensed it backing off when I asked who it was. It definitely subsided after I finished saying my say. It was tempting to ask the monk preparing the altar if the church was haunted, but I didn't.

Christy Brown

Mission Santa Barbara is located at 2201 Laguna Street, Santa Barbara.

The Old Stone Building

Just across the street from the mission in Santa Barbara is a park that few take the time to visit. But, in the expanse of weeds and dry grass are several interesting ruins.

One small structure is considered one of the most haunted in the state. The building was once listed as the Major Domo's house; now it is marked as the mission jail. This small roofless stone building is rumored to have several ghosts. Legends persist that tell of a murdered woman who frequently haunts the site.

A team of ghost hunters visited the site and conducted several experiments for an hour, or so. During their research, bizarre events took place. One of the team was pinched by something unseen. Interesting results came from their efforts. Conventional photographs taken that evening showed balls of light (orbs) floating about.

One team member used a pair of dowsing rods to attempt spirit communication. The rods crossed near the entrance. The first experiment was to try to use a code to communicate with the spirits using the rods. The researcher established that crossing rods would mean "yes" and asked the spirit to move the rods apart to mean "no." Once questions were asked in Spanish, responses came fast. When asked if this spirit was that of the murdered woman. The rods crossed – "yes". Someone on the team asked the spirit to appear – "yes." A white mist formed very slowly just outside the door. The team watched in silence as the mist began to take the shape of a woman. A cold wave suddenly swept over the room and she vanished.

The De La Guerra Adobe

Built in 1819 by Jose de la Guerra y Noriega, it is now restored as a museum dedicated to the early California.

The home was one of the largest and richest in the district and was the scene of many political and social events over the years. If local lore is true, there is a ghost in the old sala (parlor) of the adobe. It is cold in this room nd several psychics have sensed the presence of a woman in the place. Like other ghostly ladies linked to early California stories, this lady is dressed all in black. The dress of a widow. Who she is and why she is present is still anyone's guess. A woman who had reported seeing her said she was very distressed.

If you tour this site, and it's well worth a visit, be sure to see the window display where young women scratched their new married names, using the diamonds of their wedding rings.

The Casa de la Guerra Museum
15 East de la Guerra Street, Santa Barbara, California
Sunday, 12:00 noon to 4:00pm. 805.966.6961

Chumash Painted Cave State Historic Park
Painted Cave Road

The Ghosts of Painted Cave

One of the most mysterious and perhaps the most haunted places along El Camino Real is the famous Painted Cave. It was made by Chumash holy men long ago. It features symbols that may represent astrological events and their views of the afterlife. The colors used by the Chumash tribesmen in this cave indicate that they somehow acquired them from the Missions. Before that time certain colors were unknown to them.

This is one of the best painted cave sites yet discovered and one of the easiest to get too. It is located on the San Marcos Pass, north of Santa Barbara, up Painted Cave Road. Parking space is limited and access to the Cave Art is restricted by a set of steel bars. You can clearly see the beautiful designs and symbols.

Many report supernatural events are linked to this cave. People have photographed orbs near the entrance. Others have heard exotic flute music. Ghostly voices have been recorded on tape that might well be in the language of the long dead Native Spiritual Leaders (or Pahas).

The cave is also linked Valerio, a Native American rebel leader. It may have served as his hiding place for a time. He carried on a guerrilla war against the Spanish Missionaries until his capture and execution. His spirit may have returned to the cave.

For information about the cave contact or visit;
Santa Barbara Museum of Natural History
2559 Puesta del Sol, Santa Barbara, CA (806) 682-4711

GAVIOTA PASS
FREMONT - FOXEN
MEMORIAL
Here, on Christmas day, 1846, natives and soldiers
from the Presidio of Santa Barbara lay in ambush
for Lt. Col. John C. Fremont, U.S.A. and his
battalion. Advised of the plot, Fremont was
guided over the San Marcos Pass by Benjamin
Foxen and his son William, and captured
Santa Barbara without bloodshed

Bronze plaque at rest stop (PM 46.9)
North bound Highway 101
1.5 mi North West of Gaviota

Haunted Gaviota Pass

It's a place were the roadway narrows down to just a few feet. It is the place where El Camino Real moves away from the coast and into the interior of California. The long climb up the grade takes travelers to Mission Santa Inez and La Purisima. But the narrow pass is a land mark and a haunted one at that. A bronze plaque marks the location at the rest stop in the pass.

It tells the fictional account of an ambush set up by Mexican loyalists to stop Col. John C. Fremont's US Troops from moving south forcing the Americans to take a more labored approach to capture Santa Barbara. Part of the story is fiction. They reacted to a rumor about an ambush.

The ghosts date to an earlier time when a detachment of Spanish Lancers were set upon by the local inhabitants. The Spanish were forced to retreat down the road and through the pass toward the coast. For I time it looked like the Natives would win the day.

As the warriors prepared to mount a charge on the exhausted Spanish Troops a strong wind came blowing off the sea and inland. In desperation the Spanish set fire to the dry grass in the pass. The flames fueled by the wind roared up the pass. The native warriors trapped in the conflagration were burned to death.

Defeated spirits haunt the pass today. Some have reported seeing a figure who wanders alone. Local legend is that this is the chief who lead his people into a fiery defeat. There is no doubt that this is a spooky place, especially for those who visit the place at night. When the wind blows one may still hear the horrible wails of those warriors succumbing to fire.

Mission Santa Inés

Founded September 17, 1804, it was once known for the excellent saddles which were made there. Today the mission is dwarfed by the tourist town of Solvang. But this site is well worth a visit for anyone interested in the folklore of the missions of California. Many stories cling to this site. One story tells of a dark vampire that once inhabited the church when it was a ruin. The tale states that this creature will suck the blood from the toes of any hapless stranger who sleeps the night in the chapel and has the bad luck to remove his shoes. Maybe the tale has its origin in the owls who once perched in the building long ago. Another legend mirrors many told in Catholic America. It tells that the statue of San Antonio, that was brought by the Spanish padres, is somehow blessed and has the power to grant one prayer. But, any prayer must be of an unselfish nature asked with a pure heart.

This quiet place wasn't always so peaceful, for it was here in 1824 that the Great Revolt started. The Chumash native converts grew tired of the cruel treatment afforded them by the Spanish soldiers, and revolted in a bloody month long rampage. Another tale tells of a Chumash woman who warned the padres of the uprising, saving many lives. One legend says she was buried under the altar in a special site reserved for padres and political leaders. Maybe it is this woman who haunts the grounds of the old church. Some say that they feel her presence near the old laundry basin. People say that tape recordings made at the cemetery and laundry area always seem to pick up stray whispers, and the mournful wail of a Native American flute . The site is calm now but, if its memories do re-play to the visitor, this should be a very haunted site indeed.

Mission Santa Inés
1760 Mission Drive, Solvang. Open daily.

"I've heard a lot of different things about the old Mission. The tale of a monk who walks through the gardens in the mornings and evenings. There is a story about a horseman who rides around the place. Things falling down in various rooms (one in the pottery shed; some in the sacristy). We've had people complain of cold spots; very frigid areas at times when they shouldn't be. We have had a few people here who will not lock up the cuartel. They're afraid of the cuartel because of things they have felt. I've felt apprehensive at times and yet I confronted my feelings and made friends with what ever is here."

Ranger Steve Jones

Staff at La Purisima State Historic Park

Mission La Purisima

This is perhaps the most haunted of all the missions of California. La Purisima was founded December 8, 1787, by Fray Fermin Lasuen. The 11th mission established in California, it was re-built after its destruction by earthquake and flood in 1813. Today the Mission complex is restored and open as a museum of the early history of California. It is operated by the State of California. Walking the grounds can be haunting experience. La Purisima is home to many ghost stories.

A tale is regularly heard that tells of a phantom black rider that gallops past the 18 fluted columns of the padre's quarters at dusk. Some say it is the ghost of the notorious bandit, Joaquin Murietta, guarding a great treasure buried under one of the brick pillars. Maybe are story is just a old legend, but history does record that outlaws used the place as a hideout after it was abandoned by the church. There are many visitors that report hearing hoof beats though there are not horses immediately in the area.

The building that once housed the old jail is said to have a ghost. Stories tell of two young vaqueros who loved the same woman. During a fiesta at the mission, one caught the eye of their senorita with his fancy riding skills. His jealous rival devised a plan to rid himself of the competition once and for all. He lured him into the old adobe building, and stabbing him to death. He hid the body under part of a fallen wall and tried to leave the area. He later perished trying to cross the rain-swollen Santa Clara River near Ventura. He was pulled down, horse and all, by the sucking quicksand. The spirit of the murdered man is still said to haunt the jail chamber eternally incarcerated there for his crime. The old guardhouse and jail can be icy cold and have a history of odd events right up to present time.

Perhaps the reason so many ghosts haunt this site might well be the bloody Native Revolt of February 1824. It started at Mission Santa Inez, spread to Santa Barbara and then La Purisima.

Initially the uprising didn't involve the church; it focused on the soldiers and excessive taxes. The padres were left at peace. The conflict resulted in several Spanish travelers being killed. The rebels barricaded themselves in the Mission and held out for almost a month. They mounted two small cannons in the church and literally turned the mission into a fort.

The Spanish sent a force with cannons to attack the rebels. A successful bombardment caused one of the rebel cannons to explode. Over twenty natives were killed. The spirits of the slain could haunt this place now. Pockmarks from the battle are said to still exist on the pillars today.

The old corridor has a cold spot near the entrance to the padre's chapel and the old church is icy cold near the confessional. People have experienced odd results when using dowsing rods in this location. The rods can locate areas of psychic disturbances and identify places that have ghosts. A women doing research with rods in the church suddenly felt powerful hands seize her wrists. There was no one was else present yet she was pulled directly into the wall by someone or something.

The altar is the grave of one of the padres. Some believe he is a ghost that wanders here. Strange things have happened when people pause near the grave site.

An investigator was using the rods to communicate with a spirit through a simple "yes" or "no" code. She asked if the ghostly Native American spirit would prove he was present by doing something. She suggested he move the curtain on the restored confessional. She watched closely as something like a hand moved the cloth. The booth was empty. Was it a draft or the soul of a long dead warrior who died defending his family and home from injustice?

"He looked like Ben Franklin in drag" the ranger smiled as he tried to describe the phantom he had seen in the padre's quarters of La Purisima.

He had been stationed at this park for a number of years and though he had heard all of the stories of the mysterious monk, he had never experienced anything directly himself. While checking the restored room one night at closing, he saw the long haired elder sitting on a bed.

"He looked real to me" recalled the ranger. He thought it was a visitor – until he vanished.

The phantom was wearing a white robe which the witness at first mis-identified as a dress. His identity is of little doubt. The age of the image with his long white thinning hair indicate that he could only be Fray Payeras, the priest who worked so hard to build the mission so long ago.

Payeras is the only padre buried at the mission and linked to much of its history. Other park rangers have seen a ghost monk in the padres bed. The padre's ghost isn't always seen but more often the covers on the bed are messed up as if someone has laid there. Perhaps a phantom siesta?

When visiting this place, be sure to bring a camera and to permit yourself enough time to explore the many buildings at the historic park. Walk its many lonely trails. This Mission is a place where

Mission San Luis Obispo

Founded September 1, 1772 by Fray Junipero Serra. It is the fifth mission established in California.

It is now restored in the downtown plaza of the town. Like all of the missions, this place also has a ghostly figure wandering the grounds. He has been seen by visitors to the mission in the broad daylight of afternoon.

One psychic was drawn to a distinctive painting near the altar. All alone, she heard flutes playing in the chapel. They were hollow-sounding like primitive flutes. "There were more than one" she recalls today "at least three or four. They were playing a slow sad sounding song." The strange concert lasted two or three minutes and witness was checked that there were no musicians in the choir loft. "I have never heard anything like it before or since" she admits. She isn't alone.

In 1998, another visitor heard a hushed whisper in the church. She described voices that sounded like a padre was hearing someone's confession. "It was Spanish" he recalls, "but it wasn't coming from the confessionals. It was loud ...you could make out every word and it echoed. The witness was asked what was the mysterious voice saying? He replied "I don't know, I don't speak Spanish."

Mission San Luis Obisbo is located at 751 Palm Street, San Luis Obispo.

61

Mission San Miguel Arcángel

Founded July 25, 1797, by Fray Fermin Lasuen and stands as California's 16th mission.

This mission was the site of the worst mass murder in the early history of the state. Legend holds that a great treasure is concealed in the mission grounds. During the Gold Rush, the mission was operated as an Inn by an Englishman named John Reed. He amassed a great fortune, hiding his wealth somewhere on the premises. In 1849, outlaws attacked the Inn, killing Reed and 13 men, women, and children who were staying at the mission. The bandits frantically searched the mission, seeking the hidden gold, but were unable to locate the treasure. It remains lost to this day. The murderers were captured and shot. The dead were buried in a mass grave at the mission. Many have felt a persistent cold spot in the old cemetery. One psychic believes that the ghosts wander because they were not given the full rites of the Roman Catholic Church. One visitor, Debra L. Christenson , visited the site and psychically saw blood on the walls of the rooms and felt the pain of those killed so long ago. She even felt the sensation of bleeding from her back. After leaving the bleeding stopped and only a small red spot was visible on her skin as if she had somehow formed a psychic link with one of the victims. It is mysterious indeed. Many tales of a ghostly lady in white were told at the turn of the century. The woman is thought to be Mrs. Reed, one of the victims slain on the night of terror.

While touring the mission, do step into the old church. It is best known for the brilliant murals painted by the Spanish artist Estevan Munras. The decorations feature simulated balconies, doors and archways. Above the altar is a unique all seeing eye of God, a symbol found on our American dollar bill. Does the eye of God still watch visitors at the mission?

Mission San Miguel, 775, Mission Street, San Miguel.
Open daily 10 am to 5 pm.

The Rios Caledonia Adobe

Not far from the old church in San Miguel stands the historic Rios-Caledonia Adobe.

It was built by Petronilla Rios and used as a home, stagecoach stop, hotel, tavern, schoolhouse, mattress factory and tailor shop. With so varied a past it is perhaps expected that this building should have a supernatural history. Many believe the place is haunted. This story is but one of several:

> *I took my parents on a tour of the old Mission San Miguel, then we stopped at the Rios-Caledonia Adobe down the street. My mother and I were in an antique shop when my father took a self guided tour. He was the only one in the museum, except for a person typing away in the office. He stopped at the office, and saw that the room he heard the typing from was part of the museum, with iron bars over the entrance. In the room were several antiques, one of which was an old typewriter. My father is one of the most logical people I know, and he doesn't believe in ghosts. I think he has since changed his mind.*

> *Joyce Davantzis*

Mission San Antonio de Padua

This is one of the most mystic places in all California. Founded by Fray Junipero Serra on July 14, 1771, it was California's third mission. It is located in a lonely valley, surrounded now by the vast Hunter-Legget Military Reservation. The place has an atmosphere that must be felt at dawn or dusk and there are stories of a ghostly padre. Perhaps it is the shade of the pious Fray Buenaventura Sitjar, OFM, who labored here for 57 long years. He became California's first linguist by compiling a 400 page grammar and vocabulary of the language of the Mutsun Indians, so they could learn of the Christian faith in their own tongue. Perhaps the most curious pair of artifacts at this mission are two carved wooden heads. Legends claim that they are the figureheads from sailing ships brought by sailors as an offering after storm-tossed voyages around the Horn. They stand sentinel now, watching out over the fields before the mission church where Native converts once labored.

If there is one story that clings to the mission, it is the tale of the phantom headless horsewoman, seen riding toward the mission on moonlit nights. The tale is one of greed, bloodshed and horror. A yankee miner left the goldfields during the Gold Rush. He was sick and needed someplace to recover. He reached the small hamlet of Jolon, where he was taken in by an Indian woman and nursed back to health. He married her, purchased some land, and started to farm. He built a fine adobe home and furnished it with a pot-bellied stove. He even bought her a magnificent white horse. But, the spell of gold fever came over him, and he asked his wife if he could return to the gold camps to seek the yellow metal. At last, she gave in but told him he must return in two moons (months). He left the farm with his supplies seeking wealth. At last he made a strike, but lingered month after month to work the claim. When he return, with gifts he came home late at night only to find his wife with another man! Enraged to a point of insanity, he took an ax and killed the two.

The yankee, recalled his wife telling him of the tribal belief that the body must be buried in one piece or the spirit would never find peace, took the ax and decapitated her. He took her head with him, and as he left, he saw the white horse and killed it too! Now, they say the unhappy lady rides the roads near the old mission seeking her head. One account tells of a group of soldiers from the nearby military base encountering the headless horsewoman on the road to the mission. They pursued the headless apparition in a Jeep all the way to the front of the mission, where it vanished before their eyes. It would not be the last time the mysterious lady would make her presence known to the military men at the base. Sometimes , rather than seeing the glowing specter, they just hear the unearthly hoof beats of the horse! I know this mission is haunted, because I saw one here!

Mission San Antonio de Padua, Mission Creek Road, Jolon ⭐

Mission Soledad

Some say that the number 13 is cursed. The number forever stained by the Last Supper, when Jesus dined with his 12 followers and told them that one of his trusted associates would betray him. Even in our secular age, many buildings do not have a 13th floor, and the number has an evil connotation with Friday the 13th seen as the unluckiest of all days. Perhaps there is some truth to the age-old superstition, because the 13th mission founded in California proved to be plagued by bad luck. Established on October 9, 1791 by Fray Fermin Laseuen, it stands today as a haunting and crumbling ruin. A small reconstructed chapel is all that remains of the Mission Soledad. Its history is unique in that it is the only mission named by the native people. During the 1769 Don Gaspar de Portola Expedition, Fray Juan Crespi tried to talk to one of the friendly Indians he met at this site. The native replied with a word that sounded like "soledad", the Spanish word for loneliness. At first the mission prospered with the rich soil and water. But the curse on the place seemed never far away. An epidemic took many lives at the mission, then floods and starvation. Even visitors were not immune. Spanish Governor Jose Joaquin de Arrillaga died here in 1814, during a tour of the missions, and was buried beneath the church floor. Fray Vicente Francisco de Sarria starved to death at the lonely mission in 1855. He had given his own meager rations to the natives and fell into a coma while saying Mass before the altar! The Indian converts carried his body all the way to San Antonio Mission on a stretcher for proper burial. With his death, the mission was abandoned. Is it any wonder that rumors say it is his ghost that wanders the adobe ruins late at night? There could be some evidence that the ghostly tale is true. A tourist visiting the place and photographing the chapel took a picture that shows a phantom image to the left of the altar. The image wasn't seen until the photograph was developed. Some say, when they photograph

67

All that is left of the thirteenth mission's main building.
Misión Nuestra Senora Dolorosisima de la Soledad

The Ghosts of Old Monterey

The ocean side community of Monterey was the capital of Spanish and Mexican California. There are several well known stories about the historic and haunted adobe buildings in the old town.

The Robert Louis Stevenson House is said to be haunted by a lady in a long black dress. The building was once the French Hotel and it was here that writer Robert Louis Stevenson spent several months in 1879 before moving on. He did pen two short works here including "The Old Pacific Capital." The ghost who haunts the place isn't the famed author of "Treasure Island' and "The Strange Case of Dr. Jekyll and Mr. Hyde." It is said to be an elderly woman on the second floor nursery, reclining in a rocking chair. Some say she is the nursemaid named Mrs. Girardin who was here to watch over the children of the house during an epidemic. She spent day after day caring for them and she became sick. Thinking only of her young charges until she worked tirelessly caring for the children but she grew so ill that she died. Sometimes footsteps are heard near the nursery room. The old adobe hotel is now a museum open to the public and it displays many items linked to the writer Stevenson.

The old Sherman Adobe is where a phantom is seen near the well in the rear yard. Now a museum, the house once was the home of General William T. Sherman of Civil War fame or infamy. The ghost is believed to be the spirit of a man who was murdered and tossed down the well.

The historic Monterey Customs House is also in the old town. The ghost of a man working on the second floor of the old place has been seen along with several comments from visitors about cold spots and spooky tingles.

Stevenson House State Park
536 Houston Street, Monterey, CA 93940 (408) 649-2836. ✪

"Cold Spots indicate the presence of a ghost. Do not disturb them, they are but shadows of the past and they will not harm you."

Debbie Senate
Psychic

Mission Carmel

Founded by Fray Junipero Serra June 3, 1770 as California's second mission, this place is best known as the final resting place of the saintly Fr. Serra. Some even believe he returns here each year to sing the mass on San Carlos Day to a mission church filled with the ghosts of Spanish and Indian converts. Serra never saw the present stone church that was begun in 1797, 13 years after his death. The ghost of Serra may well be folklore. One of the most persistent apparitions is that of a man mounted on a horse riding past the mission heading towards Monterey. Those who have seen the figure describe a man with a cape and dressed in the uniform of an 18th Century Spanish officer. Some believe he is the royal messenger, killed by rebellious Indians as he was trying to deliver important dispatches to the Governor.

A tale of vast riches is linked to San Carlos Mission. This legend tells of the Indians of this mission who operated a gold mine located near the mouth of the Carmel River. The location of the mine shaft is lost to history and according to legend, still holds a great treasure in gold ore.

Other tales speak of ghostly Indians and moving cold spots in the picturesque cemetery where thousands lie buried. In the cemetery there is a tombstone honoring a remarkable mission Indian known as "Old Gabriel" who lived to the age of 151. In his long life he is credited with having five wives! Some historians dispute the reported age, insisting he actually lived only to the age of 140!

Gabriel, a Native convert, was baptized in the new faith by Fr. Serra himself. Perhaps Gabriel's ghost wanders the grounds enjoying the cool winds that come in from the Pacific. This is a special place where all who are interested in the history of California must come to marvel at the accomplishments of the padres.

Mission Carmel is located at
3080 Rio Road, Carmel.

MISSION SANTA CRUZ
Misión la exaltación de la Santa Cruz

Mission Santa Cruz

There is little wonder why this place is haunted, this mission is known for a terrible murder! It was founded August 28, 1791 by Fray Fermin Lasuen as the 12th mission. The soil was good and there was every reason this mission would become one of the more prosperous settlements in the chain. It was not to be, as this mission seemed founded under a curse. Problems seemed to come at every turn, from unsavory settlers established not far from the mission settlement, to earthquakes and floods. In 1812, this mission was the site of California's first murder mystery, when Fray Andre Quintana was murdered by mission Indians. At first it was believed he had died of natural causes, until the padre was exhumed and a simple autopsy (California's first) performed at the order of the governor. They didn't need to be forensic experts to see that part of the missionary's skull was crushed. In the investigation that followed, it was determined that Quintana was an ex-military man, who ran the mission with iron discipline. His strict ways were too much for the Native Americans who, in desperation, plotted his death. The findings of the court were interesting, in that they determined that the priest was at fault for failing to teach his charges right from wrong. The seven Indians involved in the murder were punished by flogging and released.

Today a small replica of the mission, a third the size of the original, stands near the site of the church. It was built to replace the original damaged by an earthquake in 1858. The ghostly monk has been seen from time to time walking near the church. Perhaps it is the ghost of Quintana, cursed for his stubborn ways to walk this site until the end of the world. The ghost is said to even wander through the old Casa Adobe (Rodriguez Adobe), built in 1824, and now open as a museum. It was once part of the mission complex and is the last bit of the mission to survive.

Mission Santa Cruz, 144 School Street, Santa Cruz. ★

73

Here lived and wrought one whom they called
The Holy Man, The Prophet, Saint
Beloved Magin Catala
Whose life, 'tis said, was without taint.

"Mission Santa Clara"
By Minnie M. Tingle

"You wanted to know about experiences at (California)
missions. Santa Clara University's Mission is basically the
church cathedral and the outside burial ground of the old friars
who founded the mission. A friend and I had gone there during
the day to check out the place. This was about 4 pm. Since it's
just a few blocks from where I live, we just walked over. We
went into the cathedral, which is open to the public during
regular hours, and there was no one there. The beautiful altar
was breathtaking. We had seen a man sitting on the left side of
the pews way up in front. We didn't think anything of him and
just went about our business of taking the pictures we took and
then headed toward the door to go outside to see the burial
ground. My friend had decided she wanted a few more pictures
and said she would meet me there. That is the only door to go in
and out of that we were aware of and when she went back in,
the little man was gone. She looked around and then came
outside the door and yelled to me to come to her. I did and she
told me the story. We went back in and looked around and
while we don't know if there is another place to leave the
church, we couldn't find one."

Gloria Young
Santa Clara.

Mission Santa Clara de Asis

The move to name Fray Junipero Serra as a saint is well underway, with only a few elements remaining before his canonization, but there was another man who was thought equally holy among the early Franciscan Padres of California. In the 19th Century his cause was seen by some as greater than Serra's. He is buried here at the eighth mission founded on January 12, 1777. Some see him as one of the un-canonized saints of Spanish California; Fray Magin de Catala. Known as "The Holy Man of Santa Clara," he had the uncanny ability to foretell the future. In a sermon delivered in 1830, he declaimed: "At the place now called Yerba Buena there shall one day arise a great and populous city. The city will flourish and its inhabitants will become rich and powerful, and when at that height of its prosperity, it will perish by earthquake and fire." Yerba Buena is now called San Francisco and, in 1906, it was indeed destroyed in a terrible earthquake and fire. The Native converts saw Catala as a living saint. Once two Indians reported that they observed Fray Magin levitating several feet off the floor while praying before a large crucifix in the church. During confession he would tell them of the sins they had left out or forgotten. There was a movement to have Catala canonized in 1884, but his cause has weakened over the years, instead the sainthood of Fray Junipero Serra has been sought. In life he was known for his piety. He fasted everyday until noon. He never ate meat, eggs or fish, making him perhaps California's first vegan. Many believe that the saintly Magin visits the mission in spirit form just before important holy days, just to make sure everything is going well. Psychics who visit Santa Clara seem drawn to the large crucifix where Catala prayed and a strange aura, or field of energy, seems to hover near this artifact. Before his death, Magin is rumored to have exorcized a haunted roadway, The Alameda (Beautiful Way), that was thought to have been infested with demons. In the move to grant sainthood to Catala, a prayer was written long ago. A copy can be found at the gift shop of the

75

mission. If you have need of a miracle or divine intervention maybe Catala might be inclined to help. The special prayer reads as follows:

O God, who didst send Thy holy servant, Father Magin Catala, to preach thy gospel to the Indians, and didst inspire him to glorify thy Blessed Name among them by example of his eminent virtues we humbly beseech Thee to honor him on earth with the testimony of miracles performed through his intercession; to grant to us by his merits all manner of blessings and to fill our minds with the light of Thy truth; that walking always in the way of Thy Commandments, we may come to eternal union with Thee; Through Christ Our Lord. Amen.

The Mission now stands as part of the Santa Clara University and little remains of the church where Catala once labored and prayed. Only the storeroom and some walls remain, but the re-constructed chapel (built in 1928), is based upon the original, with its painted facade and distinct bell tower. Try to visit in the late afternoon and seek out the spot where the holy Catala once prayed so hard he floated in the air!

Mission Santa Clara de Asis is located at Santa Clara University on the Alameda between Bellomy & Franklin Streets.

Mission San Jose

Founded by Fray Fermin Lasuen on June 11, 1797. Today this mission has been faithfully restored to its original grandeur. At one time 6,737 Indians lived, worked and died here. The restored church maybe was too good, because it has attracted ghostly presences. A psychic informed me that the place was haunted by a ghostly man wearing white and a reddish blanket over one shoulder. Another ghost rumored to walk these grounds is that of a Spanish soldier who slowly paces near the old padre's quarters. His slow, measured steps have been heard by visitors on rainy days. They say he is waiting to receive orders for some expedition inland. It is a fact that this mission was used as a military base for soldiers chasing running Indians attempting to leave the Spanish-controlled coastal area for the still pagan inland. From here forces were sent out to keep the warlike natives from raiding the other missions of the San Francisco Bay area.

Letter from a visitor:

> *I was visiting the Mission of San Jose in Fremont, California with my family... we took the tour of the mission and were about to go, when I felt a sudden rush of cold air on the back of my neck. I turned and saw a man with a dark beard and a tricorn hat, like they wore in the American Revolution, He had a sort of dark blue uniform jacket with silver buttons and wide lapels. He was looking at me most intensely. He smiled at me with a grin and I saw he had a tooth missing. He raised one arm slowly and became transparent, vanishing. No one else saw him that day. I guess it was about 4:30 or so.... I had the distinct impression that he thought I was someone else and wanted to tell me something.*
>
> *Elizabeth C. Garcia*

Mission San Jose stands at 43300 Mission Blvd, Fremont, California.

Mission San Francisco de Asis

The mission in San Francisco is dwarfed by other buildings now and it is hard for modern visitors to imagine what it was like when this structure was the only building as far as the eye could see. It was founded June 29, 1776, as the sixth mission in California. It was nicknamed "Mission Dolores," because of the nearby Laguna de Nuestra Senora de los Dolores. The present building was constructed in 1782. Because of the foggy climate on the peninsula, Mission Dolores was the only mission without vineyards. The fog is linked to one of the ghosts who haunts the place. The cemetery where so many early pioneers lie buried is also haunted by woman in a long black veil, who slowly drifts along, weeping on foggy and rainy days. This ghostly senorita is thought to be the widow of a prominent man murdered unjustly long ago. If the accounts from visitors are true the sad woman isn't alone because the church itself is haunted by a phantom figure of a monk who has been seen in the chapel early in the morning before the altar. Much of the early work at this mission was completed by Fr. Palou, Serra's close friend. It is thought that it was here that he wrote his biography of Serra's life, the first book written in California. The foggy climate was too much for the mission, and it never prospered. The buildings would later be rented and used as an inn called "The Mission House" and saloon in the Gold Rush era. Perhaps the ghostly presence is that of Palou who visits the place and dreams of what might have been. Best time to visit is early in the morning or late in the afternoon. Spend some time in the cemetery and read the tombstones of the past. They tell of difficult times when death was always close at hand. Perhaps you may encounter the dark shadowy form of the lady in black?

Mission Dolores is located on 16th and Dolores Streets,
San Francisco. Open daily.

"One (ghost) woman is occasionally reported sitting downstairs and spinning at the wheel. The other(woman) remains upstairs. Both are apparently quite content to have visitors through the house. People who claim to be able to see him also report an evil man...and there are old stories mentioning a murder.

Considering that the building was a speakeasy in the 1920s, a murder is not beyond the pale!"

Mrs. Margaret Goodale

Sanchez Adobe State Landmark
1000 Lindamar Blvd., Pacifica, CA 94044 (415) 355-4122

The Ghosts of the Sanchez Adobe

Mission San Francisco was established in 1776 as the sixth mission in the chain of coastal missions. The sandy soil near the new mission would not produce enough food.

By 1786, a mission station was set up where the soil was ideal for farming. Today we call this area Pacifica. The station was in the rich San Pedro Valley and provided grapes and produce for the mission. The peaceful andNative Americans were peaceful and readily joined the prosperous mission. Unfortunately, there was a price to pay for the Ohlone people. European diseases took a heavy toll. Perhaps some of the ghosts seen at this site today are the victims of those epidemics. In 1839 the land was granted by the Mexican Government to Don Francisco Sanchez. The station was expanded becoming the main house of the 8,926 acre Rancho San Pedro. A new adobe was built upon the foundation of the older mission structure. In 1862 the adobe was sold to Yankee General Edward Kirkpatrick. In 1908 it became a hotel and in the 1920s the former mission site became home to a wild road house with bootleg booze and jazz music. It became the "hot spot" for San Francisco--as in the old song from the musical Forty Second Street it was: "Where the underworld met the elite." It is rumored several murders took place here at that time.

In 1953 the old Sanchez Adobe was deemed a historic landmark and opened as a museum. It was at this time that ghosts began to be reported. A figure of a padre was recently seen by a visitor. Another tourist, taking pictures of the place, caught a number of orbs floating about the grounds. Local witnesses and visitors say at least three ghosts hover here at the Sanchez Adobe.

Mission San Juan Bautista

There is a majesty about Mission San Juan Bautista that doesn't seem to exist anyplace else in the chain of California missions. Maybe it is that it alone stands in a historic town with its own plaza. The church was founded on June 24, 1797, by the hard-working Fray F. Lasuen. It was the 15th mission established in the territory. It has the largest church in the chain of missions, taking nine years to finish. Today it is the central feature of a plaza of adobe homes, inns and stables. But this place isn't always peaceful, and one legend tells of a phantom monk in a gray robe and cowl that walks the plaza late at night, crossing past the Castro House to the ancient fountain. Here the ghost makes a sign of the cross and vanishes away. Perhaps it is the phantom of Fr. Tapis, who labored hard at this place and made it well known for the quality of the music and singing. Music is a long standing tradition at the mission. When you visit here, be sure to see the large barrel organ in the museum. It was given to the mission by English explorer George Vancouver in 1793. Legend holds that the "hurdy-gurdy" was once used to stop an attack by warlike Tulare Indians, who put off their raid to listen to the strange music. One psychic visiting the place heard the machine playing by itself!

I have several accounts of individuals who have encountered the unknown here.

The Mission is located at 2ⁿᵈ and Mariposa Streets, San Juan Bautista.

I felt it when I first stepped out of my car. This spot is haunted by something. I had come to the Mission San Juan Bautista with my girlfriend to see the place where Alfred Hitchcock had filmed his movie Vertigo. I didn't know the story of the mission, or anything about ghosts. But the feeling was there. I had felt it before at Williamsburg in Virginia, and at the Tower of London in England. It's like a pricking feeling on the back of the scalp. When I walked into the church, I was struck by the darkness of the chapel and the smells of incense. I saw the figure to one side of the altar, near the railing. It was a shape more than anything else. I think it was the spirit of a monk or priest because it seemed to have a hood on its head. It was moving across the room. I pointed it out to Valery, and she saw it too. I remember she said something like, "What the hell was that?" It was gone before it reached the other side of the room. We didn't stay very long after that.

(Name withheld)

The Mission wasn't my first choice as a place to visit, but my son was building a model of this one, and my husband thought it was a good idea to see the place. He wanted to take pictures and collect some pamphlets for the report. We took the tour, and I was in the garden when I started to feel as if I was being watched. The others were in the building at the time, looking at something, and I was alone. I had the feeling that I was someplace that I shouldn't be. I felt someone touch me on the shoulder as if to get me to turn around. I looked back and there was no one there. It sent a chill down my spine. I have been psychic all my life, and grew up in a haunted house in Fredericksburg, Virginia.

Christine B_____

5th Ave and A St, San Rafael

Mission San Rafael

This place was founded as a hospital to care for the Native converts taken ill in San Francisco. It started out as a branch mission on December 14, 1817. This assistencia became a full mission in 1823. The success of this mission can be attributed to the hard work of Fray Vicente de Sarria. Perhaps it is because that this place was a hospital that ghosts are found here. Many hospitals are known to be haunted. The icy cold encountered here may well be spirits of the Native people who died here. Illnesses like smallpox, measles, and even chicken pox took many lives. Visitors tell of several moving cold spots. If you should chance upon one of these phenomena, do not be frightened. They are just spirits of the past. Treat them with respect, and they will not harm you. Another event took place at the mission in 1832, Fr. Jose Maria Mercado led armed neophytes in an attack on visiting Indians, killing or wounding over 40. The priest was suspended for his part in this murderous encounter. Perhaps it is the ghosts of the dead natives who linger here. The present church is a reconstruction, built in 1949.

I was touring the missions with my son and daughter, and drove up from San Francisco, where I was staying with my brother's family. We arrived there in the morning and started the tour. I thought we could have lunch at Adriana's Restaurant afterwards. There isn't much to see as compared to the other missions in California, so I didn't think it would take long. It was in the chapel that my daughter said she saw a nun in the church, but I couldn't see a thing. To me it looked as if the chapel was empty. Then a cold something flowed right through me, as if someone or something was walking right through my body. It felt like I had been bathed in icy water that chilled me right to the bone. I was shivering all over. My daughter took my hand and said we should go. I just couldn't speak, but I let them pull me out of the church. It was the strangest thing I have ever felt.

Gloria T.

85

Mission Sonoma

Founded July 4, 1823, by Fray Jose Altimira. This small establishment was the last mission founded in California, and the most northern in the chain. It was the only mission founded during the Mexican period, and was helped by the donation of bells by the Russian settlers at Fort Ross. Today the mission is restored as a museum at the town where a band of American settlers flew the Bear Flag of California independence. (The independent state lasted about a month). The present church is a replica of the adobe chapel damaged in the 1906 earthquake that destroyed San Francisco. The mission shares with the other missions stories of a shadowy gray-robed monk who walks the grounds at noon during Holy Week. It is thought to be a ghostly missionary still trying to serve the parish he founded so long ago. A visitor heard chanting in the chapel one day, and when he walked in, he saw a monk, complete with hood, kneeling on the floor before the altar. He started to leave, thinking that some religious service was underway, but as he glanced back, the vision was gone.

Fr. Serra's Lost Mission

Ask any student of California history to name the first mission founded in California by Fr. Junipero Serra, and they would answer San Diego. But they would be wrong. At that time California was the name of the provence that included all of the Baja Peninsula. While establishing the land route to San Diego, Father Serra took time to establish a mission in central Baja, nearly 250 miles south of the present border with Mexico.

He founded this mission in a two-mile long arroyo that proved to be an oasis of green in a sea of desert, rock and cactus. The site had been first discovered in 1766 by the Jesuit Missionary, Father Wenceslaus . He met the natives of this place, and recommended that a mission be established here for the well-being of the native people. Father Serra founded his first California mission in the shadow of the twin peaks, named San Pedro and San Pablo. The first mass was sung on May 14, 1769, and the mission was named San Fernando Velicata. Fray Miguel de la Campa was appointed by Serra as its first padre. Father Serra met with the native people, and made sure they were presented with gifts and well treated. The new mission was given cattle and livestock, flour, soap, biscuits, raisins, figs, maize and a little chocolate.

Sierra moved on north to his date with destiny, leaving the new mission settlement with a single priest and a handful of soldiers. They first dammed up the creek to make sure that the community had a dependable supply of water. Then they began a large adobe building to serve as a chapel and cleared land for agricultural fields. In the years that followed, San Fernando Velicata would never attract a large neophyte population, but it would become an important supply station, sending mule trains of needed materials and foodstuff to the growing chain of missions established along the coast of California. Some historians write that San Fernando Velicata was indispensable to the early missions founded by Father Serra. While history records the rise of these wondrous settlements, with their lofty towers and tiled fountains, few ever mention that they were only possible because of a small, almost forgotten mission in Baja California.

In those years Fray Campa went about this monumental task, preaching and building as well as keeping records of his successes and failures. In 1770 he had baptized 179 natives and performed 35 marriages. Fortunately, there were no recorded deaths at the new mission. The following year he recorded 181 baptisms and 47 marriages and still no deaths. In 1772 the able Fray Campa was replaced by Fray Vicente Fuster and Fray Jose Angel Fernandez de Somera.

That year they performed 48 baptisms, 55 marriages and no burials.

In 1773, the missions of Baja California, including San Fernando Velicata, were transferred from Father Serra's Franciscan order to the Dominicans. An inventory of the mission proved how busy the Franciscan Missionaries had been. The church was completed, and stood 41 by 19 feet with a thatched roof and three windows. There was an adobe altar and a number of silver chalices, salvers, baptismal dishes, censers and a small silver bell. The padres' quarters was 61 by 19 feet, with four rooms, linens, kitchen utensils and a small library. The storehouse held pots and pans, tools, saddles, and horse tack, as well as 200 candles.

The soil, though poor, had yielded 364 sacks of wheat and barley that season. Four ranches established around the mission were also doing well with buildings of adobe, wells and corrals for livestock.

With the administration of the Dominicans, the traffic between the California and Baja missions increased, bringing with it the epidemics of European disease that decimated the native people. In 1818, the Dominicans abandoned Father Serra's first mission, leaving the adobe buildings to slowly melt back into the earth from which they had been made. Today the little mission of San Fernando is little more than a few adobe walls standing forlorn in the remote wasteland of Baja. But, the humble ruins are not at peace, and, like the others this place is haunted as well by a lonely woman dressed in a long white dress. She is said to be a ghostly woman waiting for her lover to return from his journey to Upper California. She waits in vain, because he was killed before he could come back to marry her. This hapless spirit is seen walking the grounds at dusk. If you should happen to see her you can tell she is a ghost. Why? The ghost lady has NO FACE!

With plans to elevate Father Serra to sainthood someone should think of restoring his first California mission. The small mission that made possible the celebrated "Rosary of Coastal Missions" that was the birth of our Golden State. The forgotten mission should be given its overdue recognition, and be reconstructed to all of its humble glory as a strategic outpost on an important trail.

The Ghosts of the Lost Missions of California

Most of us know of the twenty-one Missions of California but most of us would be surprised to learn that once there were two more missions in the Golden State. The two lost missions were not established along the Pacific Coast. The two were built on the California side of the Colorado River near Yuma, Arizona.

Perhaps they are overlooked by many history books because both missions ended in with terrible loss of life in one horror filled night. These mission ruins are haunted.

Originally the two missions were the brain child of a most remarkable padre, Fray Hermencildo Francisco Garces. He devised the overland trail to link coastal California to central Mexico. Because of his efforts, Mexican settlers populated the start up settlement of San Francisco, the event is referred to as the Anza Trek of 1776. His progress took him near the Colorado River where he encountered the Yuma people. He developed a good relationship with the indigenous community and eventually converted their chief, Palma. He urged for the missions to be built as conversion of the community and their acculturation into Spanish life was Spain's forgone conclusion. The Yuma were a well organized society and had long had the ability to protect their way of life and a history of success at doing so. History now tells us that delaying expansion would have been more prudent.

Fray Junipero Serra, in California, urged that the Colorado River Mission projects be stopped before they were even built. He believed that the Spanish should focus their efforts on the California coast. Commandante General Teodoro de Croix and California Governor Felipe de Neve both disagreed with Serra.

The river missions layouts were to be unlike the formula used by the Franciscans. Their projects would be a Mission and a Pueblo combining soldiers, settlers, their wives and families with the mission converts. Fray Junipero Serra believed this system was flawed as the native people would be subjected to exploitation and corruption. The resulting fear of a native revolt was the reason he felt there would be little incentive for settlers to join these missions. Fr. Garces did express concern that too few soldiers would be quartered at the missions. Their opinions were overruled and both missions projects went forward. Their concern would prove to be well founded.

In 1780 Mission La Prissima Concepcion de Maria Santissima was established and eight miles downstream, along the Colorado River, Mission San Pedro y San Pablo del Bicuner was set up. For eight months things seemed to go well. A handful of Yuma did join the mission church and the settlers began to plant crops and build structures. Beneath the drone of daily life was a building undercurrent of anger. Arrogant settlers and soldiers undermined the work of the padres. Many treated the mission converts as slaves. The outcome would be disaster.

An expedition group headed to California crossed the lands of the Yuma staying for a time at the Mission La Purisima. The expedition included forty colonists and a military escort. They allowed their animals and cattle feed in the Native American's fields. This gesture proved to be the last straw. July 18, 1781 Chief Palma attacked both missions and the military camp. The co-coordinated assault caught the Spanish by surprise. Most of the members of the missions were murdered outright. A few of the women and children were spared to serve as slaves of the Yuma. Only one man escaped the nightmare. It was speculated that the attackers permitted him to escape to describe to the Spanish leaders what had happened and to persuade them not to consider future missions in the area. They were successful.

During that horrible night of blood, Fray Garces was killed with three other padres, murdered by the very people they thought they were helping. When the killing stopped, the Yuma saw a strange vision that unnerved them. Legend says that the warriors saw a line of several ghosts there cloths were all white and they carried lit candles, bright torches and large crosses. walking . The figures moved slowly and silently around the ruins of the Mission churches like a funeral procession. The Yuma were concerned that the ghosts might seek a terrible revenge. The vision reappeared at both locations for several nights. The Yuma community moved miles away to the mouth of the Colorado River.

Not far from the site of Mission La Concepcion, today stands the Spanish Style Roman Catholic Church of St. Thomas Aquinas. A stature of Fr. Graces bending to help a Native American stands in the flower garden of the church. The garden may appear to be a place for quiet reflection but all is not calm here. The echoes of that tragic night still hold sway. A visitor to the garden said she had sensed the presence of many men in the garden. Then, she felt their presence all around her. She was overwhelmed in the garden had to leave the church grounds. She said that she felt the phantom group was a gathering of men. Perhaps they were those who were lost when the missions fell, those who the victors saw in procession after the bloodshed? Perhaps with time the ghosts of the lost mission will find peace.

"I was driving along highway 80, not far from the bridge that crosses the Colorado into Yuma, Arizona… It was about 12:30 at night and I was trying to reach my sisters house before it got much later. I saw the figure some distance away, standing by the roadway. She was a woman wearing shapeless dress or night gown , like a muumuu. She had long dark hair and in her hands a wooden cross. It was maybe a foot long.   She stepped out from the side of the road, I swerved to avoid hitting her. Then she just vanished!"

Riverside, CA resident near mission ruins in 2000

HUNTING MISSION GHOSTS

Ghost Hunting is a fast growing hobby in America and one of the best places to start are at the old Spanish Missions of California and Adobes. I have a few tips to would-be ghost hunters and all who wish to find evidence of ghosts as part of your Mission trek.

1. Don't disturb others. Be aware of those who are at prayer. These Missions are not only historic places, but also places of worship. Please remember that men should remove hats before entering a Catholic church.

2. Take lots of pictures! Both outside and inside of the church, if allowed. Use high speed film. Tri X is good but anything over 1000 asa will work. Black and white does seem to work better. Some swear by infrared film and I have seen good results with digital cameras. Recording with analog and digital video equipment can prove valuable.

3. Use new, music-quality tapes. The best recorders for our purposes have a detachable microphone.

One of the best places to record are cemeteries. Ask questions and leave time for an answer. You may not hear anything until you rewind and play back the tape. The spirit voices will have a whispered quality to them.

4. Dowsing rods and pendulums should be used where you have privacy from public view and remember that additional information will be needed to confirm their accuracy. I have found La Purisima State Historic Park in Lompoc is a good place to try these tools.

5. Please be respectful of the every site and what ever or whoever is there. I believe a professional demeanor serves you and the ghosts best. Leave any place you go cleaner than the way you found it! Like a ghost, a ghost hunter should leave no trace behind.

6. Never trespass or visit places that are off limits! Leave money in the poor box whenever possible.

7. Researching a regions history will add greatly to your experience when visiting a historic site. Records may have stories that account for the presence of a ghost. A good ghost hunter remains skeptical but keeps an open mind.

The Haunted Mission Trail

The 650 miles of El Camino Real are a haunted highway indeed. These sites listed are but a few of the places where ghosts are said to walk.

The ghosts of the golden state trace their roots back to the first mission padres who carved a chain of outposts along the coast of California.

Do travel this highway and see if you encounter one of the many ghosts of El Camino Real-The King's Highway.

- Richard Senate -

Richard Senate

Richard L. Senate was born in Los Angeles and moved to Ventura County at the age of three. He considers himself to be a life long county resident. He attended Thousand Oaks High School, Ventura High School, Ventura Community College, Long Beach State University and The University of California at Santa Barbara. He oldest son of a painter/decorator who once worked for MGM Studios and Irwin Allen Productions. Richard has always seen the world though an artist's eyes. He is the author of six published books. Many of his works deal with the subject of ghosts and the supernatural and local history. In print currently: Ghosts of the Haunted Coast, (Pathfinder Publishing), The Haunted Southland, Erle Stanley Gardner's Ventura, and The Ghost Stalker's Guide to Haunted California (Charon press). Hollywood's Ghosts, Ghosts of Ventura, Ghosts of the Ojai and Historic Adobes of Ventura County. (Del Sol Publications) *www.delsolpublications.com*

Mr. Senate has worked for the Cultural Affairs Division of the City of Ventura and managed the Historic Tours program and the Olivas Adobe Historic Park, a nationally recognized historic house museum. He has been a teacher with the Ventura Elderhostel program since 1997 with classes on California History and the history of Hollywood. He also has lectured at California State University at Northridge, Pierce College and Ventura College. He currently resides in Ventura County.

He has appeared on numerous TV and Radio programs over the years including Sightings, the Travel Channel Specials where he has spoken as an expert on the subject of ghosts and the supernatural. His web site on the internet was one of the very first on the subject of ghosts. It is located at **www.ghost-stalker.com**